I0189426

IMAGES
of America

COTTAGE GROVE

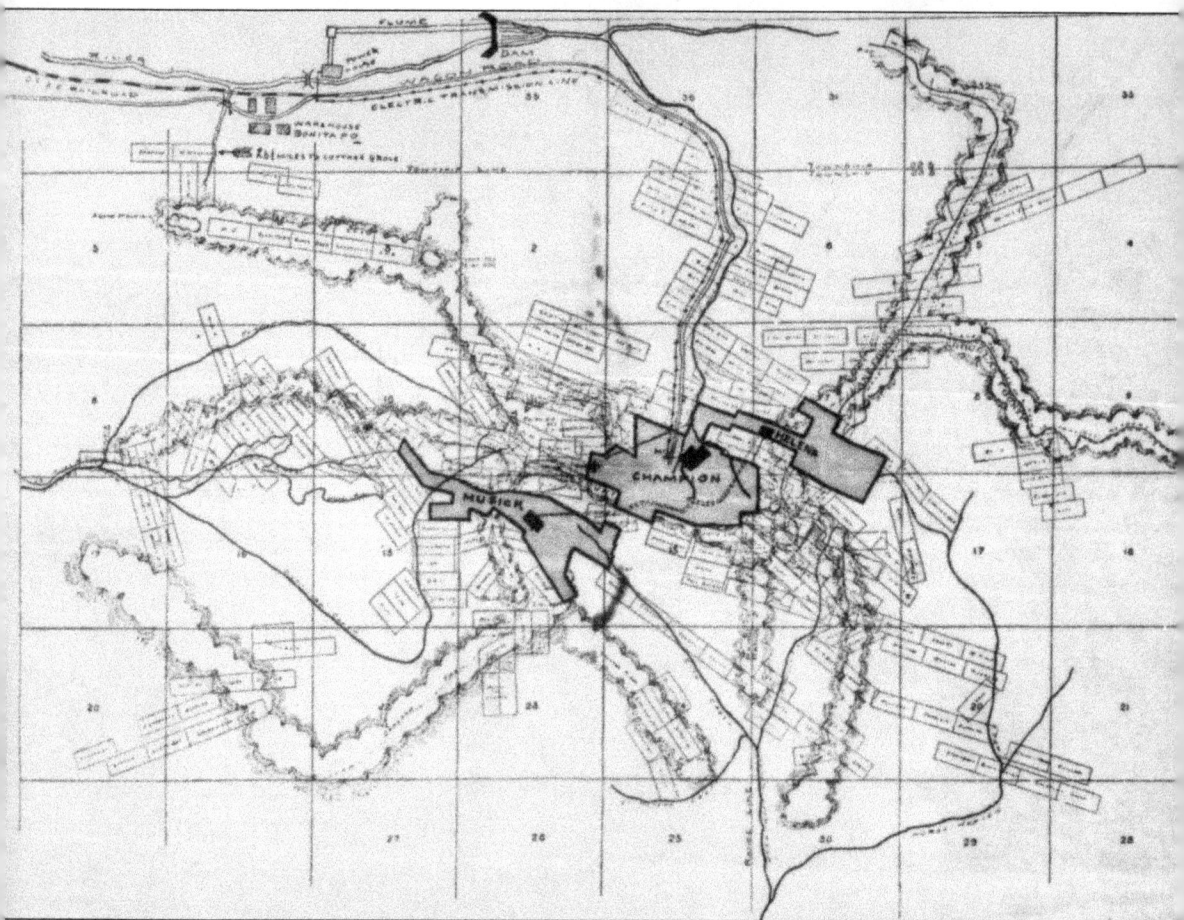

This map of the Bohemia Mountains a few years into the gold-mining boom shows the big three claims and the hundreds of standard claims scattered across the exposed ore veins. At the apex of the mining, the claims took up 900 acres. On the top of the map near the wagon road are the dam and powerhouse that provided power to the city. (CGM.)

ON THE COVER: Fred Graber and the Zinniker brothers pause work on a new tunnel for a photograph. They are beginning an adit into the mountain. Their hard work eventually paid off when high-grade ore was hit that assayed for $29,000 a ton. They ended up selling their claim to Frank Hard who started the Vesuvius Mining Company. (Both, Bohemia Mining Museum.)

IMAGES
of America

COTTAGE GROVE

Caleb and Angela Garvin

ARCADIA
PUBLISHING

Copyright © 2010 by Caleb and Angela Garvin
ISBN 978-1-5316-5316-3

Published by Arcadia Publishing
Charleston, South Carolina

Library of Congress Control Number: 2009937672

For all general information contact Arcadia Publishing at:
Telephone 843-853-2070
Fax 843-853-0044
E-mail sales@arcadiapublishing.com
For customer service and orders:
Toll-Free 1-888-313-2665

Visit us on the Internet at www.arcadiapublishing.com

*To the Cottage Grove pioneers who left behind their stories and images,
and to the volunteers who work so hard to preserve our history*

CONTENTS

ACKNOWLEDGMENTS

Authors of this book would like to acknowledge and extend our heartfelt gratitude to the following persons and associations who have made its completion possible: we would like to sincerely thank the ungrudging efforts put in by a large number of individuals working at the Cottage Grove Historical Society (CGHS), the Cottage Grove Museum (CGM), the Bohemia Mining Museum (BMM), and Melvin Gowing's collection of photographs (MGC). Special thanks go to Marcia at the historical society; Marie and Joanne at the museum; the descendants of the Brumbaughs for sharing family stories and pictures; and Melvin Gowing, who lent us his knowledge and photographs of our railroad history. I would like to express our gratitude to the many people who saw us through this book, those who provided support, talked things over, offered comments, and allowed us to quote their remarks. Last and not least, thanks to all the local residents of Cottage Grove who helped us with the historical stories of our town and whose names I have failed to mention and to our family and friends.

INTRODUCTION

Cottage Grove is located in the Southern Willamette Valley. With its small-town atmosphere and close proximity to the Eugene area, the Cascade Mountains, and the Oregon coast, Cottage Grove's popularity has continued to grow. Cottage Grove has come a long way since the first locals, the Calapooya Indians, lived there. The area was known by the natives to be a plentiful hunting ground with mild winters. Even the Klamath Indians would make the long journey over the rugged Bohemia Mountains to fish at Wildwood Falls on the Row River. The first settlers came to Cottage Grove in 1848 via the Oregon Trail and then later, the Applegate Trail. After the settlers came to the area, they blazed a trail east following the Row River. It became known as the Parker Trail. After gold was discovered, many used this trail to gain access to the mines that spotted the mountainside.

The city of Cottage Grove received its moniker from the first postmaster Greenberry C. Pearce. At that time, the postmaster's house was the post office. One day, while looking at his cottage, which stood in an oak grove, he dubbed it Cottage Grove. However, the city was not always known as Cottage Grove. In the past, the city has been known by a few different names. The first to stick was the nickname "Slab Town." This stuck for a long time even after the "Cottage Grove" Post Office was built, primarily because during the wet winters the streets were so muddy they were impassible by wagon. To remedy this situation, wooden slabs were laid out to facilitate smoother crossing. In 1893, the east and west sides of town were feuding. The east side petitioned the governor and was granted a township in 1895, which they named Lemati. Lemati was a slang word meaning "the mountain," although it is often translated as "peaceful valley." At one point, a sign hung at the railroad station with three different names. When the train would stop, the railroad conductor would call out, "Slab Town, Cottage Grove, Lemati."

The post office was a bone of contention between the feuding Cottage Grove and Lemati. After the arrival of the railroad, it worsened to the point where the citizens of Lemati refused to let the railroad unload the mail for Cottage Grove. As a result, the postmaster for Cottage Grove had to hitch up an old buckboard and travel to Latham to retrieve the mail. One side wanted the post office to be near the railroad station, but the others did not want it moved at all. Whoever happened to be appointed postmaster moved it to their home or business location. One day, the marshal of Lemati was arrested in Cottage Grove while picking up his mail. He had forgotten to remove his badge before crossing the river. Soon after, Lemati sent a request to the government to move the post office 600 feet east. After permission was granted, John Durham and Oliver Veatch took a team to the west side in the middle of the night and dragged the post office back across the river to Lemati. It was thought to be a prank but ended up being a satisfactory solution for both sides.

Another great story begins with the installation of the first streetlights—kerosene lanterns—placed on posts down the street in Cottage Grove. J. B. Mosby (who was slightly drunk) decided he would have some fun by riding his horse down the streets while knocking the lights off the posts. When the marshal started after him, Mosby leaped off his horse and headed for the river. Marshal Damewood grabbed Mosby's coattail, and they both went into the river. After Mosby was soused under the water a few times, he finally gave up. The stunt ended up costing Mosby a hefty sum of $90.

It was an eventful time for both sides of the town, but peace prevailed and eventually, after a few years of feuding, in 1899 the city once again had only one name, Cottage Grove.

Early settlers from the Upper Coast Fork went into the Bohemia Mountains in early 1858. In 1863, James "Bohemia" Johnson, who was on the lam from the law in Roseburg and hiding out in the mountains, discovered gold near his camp on City Creek. After following the river back to civilization, word soon got out and the gold boom ensued. Mining was one of the main reasons for the boom of Cottage Grove. Gold drew people to the mines, many different treasures in the mountains attracted attention from all around, and boomtowns sprung up all over the area. This gave Cottage Grove some of its first post offices, schools, hotels, and some of its oldest cemeteries. A wagon road was built in 1895 from what is now known as Culp Creek up Sharp's Creek to the Painted Post Ranch, where a horse and mule trail was built into the mining district. There were over a dozen different mines started and 2,000 claims were filed almost overnight.

Much of the success of mining in the Bohemia District was due to the fact that heavy equipment could be manufactured a short distance away, making for easier shipping to the mining district. Hammond Manufacturing Company of Portland, Oregon, manufactured most of the stamp mills and jaw crushers that were used in the district. The jaw crusher reduced the ore to gravel-sized chunks. Then the stamp mill reduced the ore to a powder fine enough to release the gold from the matrix.

Throughout the years, a few major mines have stood the test of time. The Champion Mine had two large mills constructed on the property. The first one was about one quarter of a mile down Fairview Mountain from the main adit. The period of greatest production was during the 1890s until the early 1900s. The Champion Mine has changed names and is now known as the Morning Star. The claim is still giving up gold for those willing to expend the energy to mine it.

The Helena Mine was one of the oldest mines in the Bohemia District and the ore was unusually high in gold content. The lower tunnels and the Helena milling complex were located about 500 feet below the ridge. Early production figures from the Helena Mine indicated $1.5 million recovered in gold.

James C. Musick discovered the Musick Vein in 1891, and he erected a five-stamp mill on the property in 1892. The Musick Mine is located on the slope of the Bohemia Mountain, and the main adit is located at an elevation of 5,000 feet. The Musick Mine was the second mill to be built in the district. Bohemia City was located at the Musick Mine, and the original camp consisted of a 30-man bachelor bunkhouse, a cookhouse, four family homes, a hotel, a store, and a livery barn. Bohemia City was by far the largest community to be established in the district. It was occupied year-round and reportedly had a population upwards of 1,800 people.

The Noonday Mine, originally called the Annie Mine, was named after the daughter of Dr. W. W. Oglesby and was the second mine to operate in the district. The mine was situated near the summit of Grouse Mountain overlooking the Horse Heaven Basin.

The Vesuvius Mine is located on the west slope of Fairview Mountain. The Zinniker brothers and Fred Graber bought the Vesuvius Mine in May 1899. Several of the Vesuvius Mine veins were discovered before 1895. In 1902, they hit high-grade gold that assayed at 1,450 ounces to the ton of ore. They sold out to Frank Hard who started the Vesuvius Mining Company. Fred Graber opened a hardware store in town with his portion of the proceeds. Many downtown businesses were started by people who obtained their grubstake in the mines. At one time, there were seven saloons on the north side of Main Street. The old Helena Saloon still stands to this day as the oldest building on Main Street. The Bookmine, a bookstore and gift shop, currently resides there. Those uninterested in cards, dancing, or alcohol, walked on the other side. The ladies and children had small park areas and inside reading rooms to rest in while waiting for their men to take the family home.

By 1864, a railroad line was under construction in Oregon and on its way to Cottage Grove. It was welcomed by the locals since the roads where so muddy they were almost impassible during the winter months. In 1872, the railroad line finally reached Cottage Grove. As the business district grew, it moved east. When the railroad came, businesses started to develop on what is now Main Street. The railroad was the center of commerce as well as the primary form of transportation, other than stagecoach or team and wagon. In 1887, a city council was formed that still exists today.

The discovery of high-grade, oxidized ore in the Bohemia Mountains gave birth to the first short line out of the city in 1903. One miner has been quoted saying, "It was 40 miles from nowhere to nowhere through nothing." With the mining boom, the railroad was extended up to Disston, but fell a bit short of many of the mines and boomtowns. When the mining industry fell upon hard times, the logging industry was there to pick up the slack. The railroad went from hauling ore carts to pulling flat trailers filled with logs.

When the mines started to lose some of their business, the logging industries stepped in to save the city. Every valley and mountaintop was covered with old growth timber. Some of the earliest logging in Lane County occurred on the Upper Coast Fork (now the site of Cottage Grove Dam). William Payne settled the area and built the first sawmill in 1867. This was only the beginning; the logging boom lasted until the late 1980s.

While the glitter of gold drew many, the logging industry certainly provided more jobs and a greater profit. Several lumber companies started in Cottage Grove, including the Bohemia Lumber Company, which was among the largest in the world. Others were the Brown Lumber Company, Woodard's Mill, Booth Kelly Lumber Company, and the J. H. Chambers Mill. At one time, there were 23 sawmills on Row River alone. Logging has proven to be a long-term, renewable resource, providing many jobs to this day. Although the heyday of logging has passed, the thick forests will continue to provide jobs and lumber for many generations to come.

In the years before paved roads and automobiles, towns were spaced for wagons. What is now known as the Cottage Grove area was originally about 15 different towns: Walker, Saginaw, Lorane, Divide, Latham, London, Hebron, Dorena, Star, Culp Creek, Wick, Wildwood, Disston, and Rujada. Some of these have remained, while some have faded away to obscurity. We hope you enjoy this look into the past of Cottage Grove. If you happen to find yourself in town, be sure to visit the Cottage Grove Museum, the Bohemia Mining Museum, and the Cottage Grove Historical Society. Due to the format of this book, we are unable to provide a complete history of Cottage Grove. It was our intention to provide a broad overview of the history of the area. If you desire more information on any of the subjects in this book, please visit the aforementioned places for a more in-depth look into the history of Cottage Grove.

The Modern Woodmen of America stood in front of the Pacific Timber building. Off to the right side is Baker and Johnson's Feed, Provision, and Grocery Store. The Modern Woodmen is a fraternal order started by Joseph Root in 1883. It began as a benefit society to protect families in the event the main breadwinner died. (CGM.)

One

ROWING DOWN
MAIN STREET

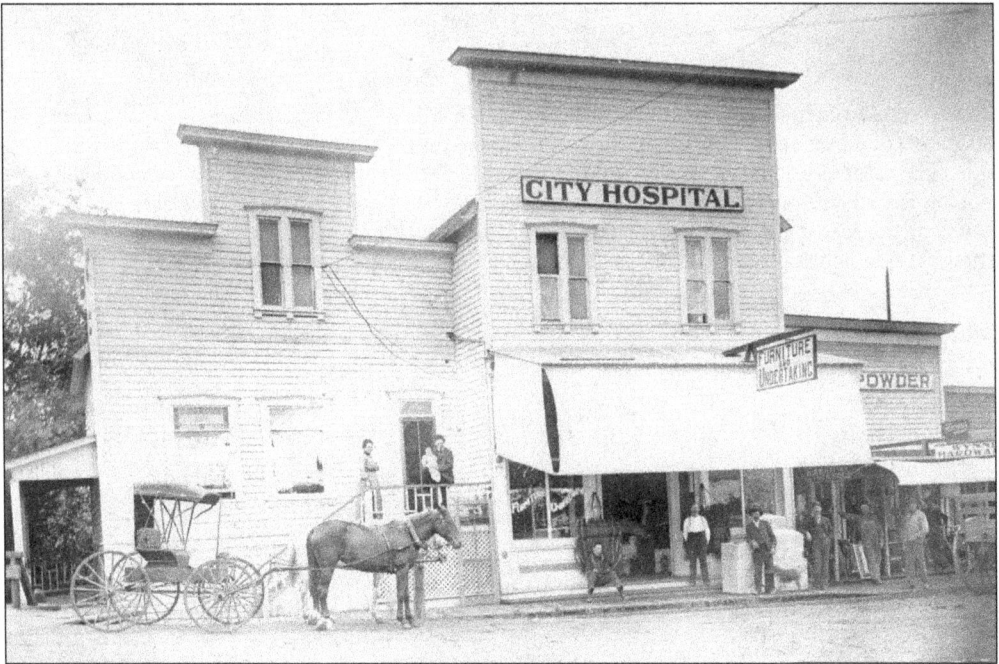

The first Cottage Grove Hospital was built on Main Street by Dr. Henry and Katherine Schleef. Dr. Schleef is shown here holding a baby with Katherine standing close by. The horse and buggy wait for the doctor to make a house call. The fee for such a call ranged from $1 to a basket of fresh farm eggs, maybe even a chicken. Stores occupied the street level of the main building, and the hospital rooms were upstairs. The doctors and their families also lived in a suite located on the upper level. Under the sign reading, "City Hospital" is a smaller sign that reads, "Furniture and Undertaking," an example of the businesses on the lower levels. (CGM.)

As more people came to Slab Town, the river came to divide the wild east side and the settled west side. The saloons and brothels were on the east side of the river and businesses were on the west side. A feud developed between the rebel rousers and the businessmen. By 1893, the feud was so bad that the east side petitioned the legislation to be incorporated as a separate town. Even with the west side fighting the petition, east Cottage Grove was granted a township. This fanned the

flames of the feud between the towns. One example of the rivalry occurred after a fire broke out and both towns sent hose crews, each one trying to outdo the other. In February 1899, Lemati and Cottage Grove incorporated into one town again—Cottage Grove. After several years, peace reigned throughout the valley, and the name Lemati was soon forgotten. (CGHS.)

MAIN STREET LOOKING EAST FROM BRIDGE, ABOUT 1902

After Lemati incorporated as a town, they chose O. F. Knox as their mayor. J. I. Jones was elected mayor of Cottage Grove with Jack Baker as the appointed marshal. Cottage Grove passed an ordinance prohibiting bicycle riding on the sidewalks and one day Marshal Baker caught the daughter of the Lemati mayor disobeying this rule. He quickly escorted her back across the bridge. The following day, Marshal Baker went to get his mail and forgot to remove his badge before crossing the bridge into Lemati. He spent the night in the Lemati jail. (CGHS.)

Bert Trask took this picture of his "Zerolene" horse-drawn wagon. It was used to deliver oil—used for heating and oil lamps—to the residents of Cottage Grove. Bert worked for the Standard Oil Company located just south of the switchyard in Cottage Grove, driving the old Zerolene wagon and later a Ford Model T delivery truck. (CGM.)

J. P. Currin's Drug Store was located on South River Road. The store was a brick building constructed in 1884. In the *Cottage Grove Leader*, an advertisement for the store read: "Anything or everything in the druggist line, wallpaper, paints, oil, varnish, and etc." The walls were filled with just about everything a person could need in those days. (CGM.)

The Lurch Brothers arrived in Cottage Grove with only the packs on their backs. The brothers built the first general merchandise store (left), just east of the bridge. The local residents would provide the merchants with different things to sell in their stores, such as fresh or canned fruit, jam, breads, and other goods. (CGM.)

As seen from this picture, the Reese-Wallace Store was a place that people could find a wide variety of items needed in their day-to-day lives along with those special occasion items. One could get a bottle of sarsaparilla along with the grain for the horses. This was a true one-stop shopping center. (CGM.)

The Hamilton-Wallace brickyard was located at the foot of Mount David. The bricks where made of clay, sand, and water, which was mulled in a mixer by a horse hitched to a long sweep. After the mud was ready, it was then poured into wooden molds and set in the yard to dry in the sun. Once a year, the bricks would be stacked together to make a kiln and then "fired." Afterwards, they would be ready for use in the local town's buildings. (Above, CGM; right, CGHS.)

In a time before mass-produced goods, the local blacksmith was a one-stop shop. He could fix wagons, make tools, shoe horses, and fix just about anything made of metal. As one might imagine, the hammering of the blacksmith was heard from dawn until dusk in an effort to keep up with demand. (CGM.)

The Bohemia Stage offered service from Cottage Grove to the mines. The livery barn offered fresh horses for the stage and a place for those passing through to feed and water the animals out of the rain. Stage drivers George McQueen and James Potts are seen here with two mounts. (CGM.)

Veatch Lawson's furniture and undertaking store (right) is pictured here with a few local men standing on the sidewalk getting some sun and fresh air. Between Lurch's store and Veatch's store, one could stop to visit the dentist. Five single lightbulbs are hung down Main Street making way for future growth. (CGHS.)

Main Street in Cottage Grove in 1906 definitely looked like a town. The streets were not as busy as they are today, but a little boy on the sidewalk (left) still wanders down the street window shopping for that new toy or waiting to have lunch with his parents at the local diner. (CGHS.)

Eagle cigar store in 1913

6th and Mains 1892-93

In the small town of Cottage Grove, water was something everyone was well acquainted with. For six to eight months during the wintertime, it would rain every day, sometimes up to several inches in an hour. With nowhere for the water to go, the streets were the first to fill up and flood. More often than not, the water would channel down the city's dirt roads. The residents would often find themselves wading through water in the road. This spurred the building of wooden sidewalks down Main Street and eventually to the construction of two dams above the city. (CGHS.)

1899 – 6th & Main St

The flooding of the town's streets was so common that the Cottage Grove Hotel stored a small rowboat on the second floor. They would carry the boat down the stairs to ferry customers between the railroad station and the hotel. After the Cottage Grove Dam and Dorena Dam were built, the flooding thankfully became a thing of the past. (CGM.)

Since the early days, the rainy season has been a way of life. For six to eight months a year, it would rain and with nowhere for the water to go, it would often flood the streets. The residents of the city would often find themselves wading through the streets in the beginning of the season and using their boats to navigate the roads toward the end of the season. (CGM.)

Another cold winter day dawns with snow in the hills and Main Street underwater once again. It seems everyone is out surveying how difficult it will be to navigate the flooded streets. It must have been very different after the dams were built and the streets no longer flooded with every rainstorm. (CGM.)

Boys will be boys and they just cannot help but play in the water. After school and when all chores were done, the flooded streets of Cottage Grove proved to be the local playground while fathers finished up work at the blacksmith shop (left). (CGM.)

The East Side Bell Tower and Fire Station were located on South Sixth Street. The bottom of the tower housed the man-drawn hose cart. After a fire, the hose would be looped over a hook in the top of the tower to dry. It was said to have taken a day to dry, after which it was laid out and rolled up. The bell from the old tower is now mounted near the present-day fire station. (CGHS.)

Firefighters had hard work in front of them when the fire bell rang. First, they would pull a two-wheeled cart alongside a hydrant. Then, they would unwind the hose, sometimes up to 500 feet long, attach it to the hydrant, and water down the fire. Even after the motor-driven trucks were available, the horse-drawn hose carts could still be found at the scene of a fire alongside the truck. (CGHS.)

In 1901, a fire drill was held in the town of Cottage Grove. Just three minutes after the alarm sounded, a cart had already been taken three blocks, the hose had been attached to the hydrant at the Christian Church, 250 feet of hose was unrolled, and a stream of water was pumping on the opposing team. (CGHS.)

On July 15, 1889, in Drain, Oregon, a Cottage Grove newspaper was printed. The *Cottage Grove Leader* was the town's first newspaper. It changed hands a few times before receiving the name *Bohemia Nugget*. In 1897, a paper messenger was established for the *Nugget*, which was a weekly paper out on Fridays. (CGHS.)

Two

CIVILIZATION AT LAST

The Crawford Hotel and the Pacific Phone Company were located in the same building. For guests, the hotel was conveniently located next to the Gray Goose Café. The owners and operators of the hotel kept an apartment upstairs for convenience—a very common practice for hotel owners at the time. (CGHS.)

F. C. Stiller established a creamery in Cottage Grove. Ice crushers and ice cream freezers were installed to supply the town with an ice cream parlor. For many of the children of the town, this was their first time tasting the dessert, and just like today, it was loved by all children. (CGM.)

Andrew Nelson gave Cottage Grove its first electric lights in the 1890s when he built on a dynamo at the waterwheel at the flour mill on Silk Creek. Nelson set up poles and strung wires all over town with lights. By 1899, he moved his light plant from the flour mill and converted it to steam. (CGHS.)

William "Billy" Cooper started the construction of the Bartell Hotel in 1908. The land was originally part of the William Shield's addition, one of the earliest subdivisions in the community of Cottage Grove. From 1911 to 1912, the Cottage Grove Post Office operated out of the west bay of the hotel. (CGM.)

Many early pictures of Cottage Grove include the Bartell Hotel (left). It was conveniently located across the street from the Stage Depot and next to Fred's Place. This is where a hotel guest and locals could stop and get a hot bowl of chili or pick up a hot dog or hamburger for 10¢. (CGHS.)

Cottage Grove's first flour mill was unique in that it used water to power its custom grinding wheels. "Legend says the owner first used the crude mill to grind feed for his hogs. Then later he began to grind grain for his neighbors." This was an advantage for the settlers and saved the locals a two-week trip to the nearest mill at Oregon City. (CGHS.)

The flour mill was built around 1860. It was water powered from the millrace, which ran from a wooden dam on the Coast Fork of the Willamette River. The millrace followed the river to the millpond and then dumped back into Silk Creek. The mill was a four-story building that was able to grind 48 barrels of flour a day. (CGHS.)

In 1909, one of the most important industries in Cottage Grove was the flour mill, which was located on South River Road and operated by George Matthews. Many tons of flour were shipped to Bohemia to provide food for the miners and their families. The locals also would trade sacks of wheat by the wagonload to the mill in exchange for a winter's supply of flour. (CGHS.)

The old gristmill on the west side of the mouth of Silk Creek turned into a full-fledged flour mill. The flour sacks sported a logo that could not be washed out no matter how much scrubbing one did. It was said that "many little children from town had a big red rose and the inscription 'Pride of Oregon' on their underwear." (CGM.)

Bert Trask drives his horse-pulled Zerolene wagon down West Main Street. On his way, he passed a parked Model T car (right) near the Star storefront that was located on the corner of Main Street and South River Road. The signs hung on the storefronts show how popular candy and tobacco was in 1920. (CGM.)

In the early heyday of automobiles, road trips were extremely popular. Unfortunately, early roads were often poorly built and maintained. Breakdowns were a very common occurrence. This tour group was pulled into town by the one automobile still in working order. (CGM.)

Cottage Grove Cannery was conveniently located three blocks south of the train depot. Most of the produce used included pears and apples that came from the Lorane Orchards. However, locals were able to make some money too since other fruits and vegetables were from local farms and gardens. Anyone who could pick berries would. A bucket of evergreen blackberries paid out around 8¢ a pound. (CGM.)

The Arcade Theater opened with J. E. Able as a proprietor. Families came to watch actors bounce around the large, black and white screen with captions across the bottom. Teenagers would sit in the balcony holding hands and eating popcorn. (CGM.)

During the 1890s, during the height of the feud between Cottage Grove and Lemati, there was a population spurt due to the mining boom. The population grew from 800 people to 3,000 in a short time. Vacant lots throughout the cities began to fill up. The Oregon Hotel was a popular stop for many newcomers on their way to the mines. (CGM.)

The Cottage Grove Hotel was built in 1901 during the mining boom. The hotel had an annex that could be reached by a covered walkway between the two upper stories. When a weary traveler arrived by train or wagon, they invariably made their way down the town's wooden sidewalks to the hotel for a good night's rest. (CGM.)

Darwin Bristow and Herbert Eakin built a general merchandise store just south of the gristmill. Eakin and Bristow's Dry Goods was a place where settlers' bounty checks could be cashed. Many old-timers kept their money in the store's safe. The establishment kept a night watchdog named after General Grant. It would soon be known as the First National Bank. (CGM.)

Machine shops were vital for many of the businesses in the area. This 1900s machine shop shows some of the equipment used in that era. The workers in the old shop would make parts for the mines and the logging industries that were belt-driven. The belts would motorize wagon-wheel hubs that moved the grinder bearings on the Landis machine or the metal lathes. (CGHS.)

The horse and buggy was still a very popular way for many to travel, however, automobiles were becoming more common. In 1908, Cottage Grove paved Main Street. With the new age of automobiles, the city received its first full-service gas station in 1921, built by Walter and Mrs. Bungex on the corner of Main and Eighth Streets. (CGHS.)

Oscar Woodson began selling Ford automobiles on River Road around 1914. He was known to deliver new cars to rural residents on a large horse-drawn wagon to keep the paint from getting scratched. Woodson's garage expanded and moved to the corner of Ninth and Main Streets in 1920. The new store had plenty of room to garage hotel guests' automobiles plus two gas pumps out front. (CGHS.)

Cottage Grove supported two banks in the early 1900s. Both of the banks were locally owned and operated. N. E. Glass had established the Cottage Grove Bank just east of the Methodist church on Main Street, between the bridge and Fifth Street. Sadly, the bank had to close its doors within a few years. (CGHS.)

This 1903 Ford Model A (rear entrance tonneau) was on display at the local bank. The Model A was the first production automobile for the Ford Motor Company. The car weighed around 200 pounds and could reach up to 30 miles per hour. Like many of the early automobiles, this one had a horse-and-buggy design. (CGHS.)

Since before the streets were paved, citizens could be seen from time to time gathering for festival parades. They might first stop by the local store to grab a soda pop from Lurch's market, then line up alongside Main Street under the only arc lightbulb in the town at the time. (CGHS.)

The first fair was sponsored by the Cottage Grove District Fair Association. Every festival included a Main Street parade that was held with horses, wagons, and buggies artistically decorated by locals. The festival included competitions, and prizes were given to the winners in categories of local farm products and livestock. (CGHS.)

Around 1890, private wells began to disappear. Two prominent citizens, R. M. Veatch and G. H. Stone, erected a reservoir on Mount David where wooden pipes were laid and hydrants were built. Water began to flow down to the town from Bennett Creek in 1892. The new water supply was invaluable to the city, as one might imagine, not only for drinking but also for fighting fires. In 1893, the feuding cut off water to the east side. A new reservoir was constructed on Emigrant Hill. (CGM.)

The area of Mount David was also a popular site for motorcycle hill-climbing races. Mount David's east face has a grade of 80 percent, which inspired some exciting races. These annual contests were sponsored by the Eugene Motorcycle Association. In 1926, there were 40 entrants who attracted a crowd of 6,000 persons. (CGM.)

Dedication Ceremonies Oil Well, Mt David
Cottage Grove Ore. Nov 9, 1923.

Wilbur McFarland and W. A. Hemenway were two west-side farmers in the area that leased 3,000 acres to Reverend Olson for his oil well. The 3,000 acres were divided into 300 units. The reverend promised the citizens they would not lose a penny if they purchased a unit. Each unit cost $1,000, however, several people could buy one unit together. It was then decided by the company to erect the derrick on Mount David. Reverend Olsen, in the long coat, is shown here at the dedication of Mount David Oil Well. He had hired the Sage and Olsen Brothers Drilling Company. (CGHS.)

Dedication of Oil Well on Mt David
Cottage Grove Ore. Nov 9, 1923.

This is the site of Reverend Olson's oil well. Olson came to town in the 1920s and convinced many residents that there was oil atop Mount David. He raised nearly $23,000, constructed a derrick, and then skipped town without producing one drop of oil and with everyone's money. The 100-foot-tall derrick stood until 1933 when it fell with a crash heard for miles. The derrick can be seen in the background of several scenes from the Buster Keaton movie, *The General*, which was shot in and around Cottage Grove in the 1920s. The remnants of the oil well are still there. An artifact of the operation, a drilling plug, was recently found and is on display in the Cottage Grove Museum. (CGHS.)

The settlement called Hebron was originally known as the Carpus Prairie. When winter storms caused the river to become impassable, the settlers were isolated. Many bridges were built and washed away by the flooding winter waters. In 1917, the Hebron Covered Bridge was built just south of the Hebron School. (CGM.)

With the Cottage Grove Dam under construction, the city's streets would be free of flooding in the winter months at long last. The dam was completed in 1942 and uprooted the townspeople of Hebron. Many of the buildings were left at the bottom of the lake to rot away with the myriad of tree stumps that dotted the valley. (CGHS.)

Three

THE PEOPLE BEHIND THE CITY

The Ferns were a Native American family well known to the area. Sam Fern was the last known full-blooded Calapooya Indian. He was known to locals as "Chief Sam." He was one of few Native Americans that were able to get a land claim—for 80 acres in the Yoncalla area—in his day. (CGM.)

Mary was a native Calapooya Indian known to many as "Indian Mary." She washed clothes for the McFarlands and the Finnertys and they often paid her in fruits and vegetables from the garden. The families said she was as strong as a man and a very good tanner. Many people enjoyed her handmade gloves. The McFarlands thought of her as family and buried her in their family cemetery. (CGM.)

Indian Mary sits among several of the local ladies that she helped out with day-to-day chores. Laura McFarland and Lora Finnerty as well as many other local ladies used Mary's laundry service until her death. Mary's house in the background shows how the resourceful could get by on very little, using bark and leftover boards for construction. (CGM.)

Samuel Brumbaugh brought his family to Oregon from Indiana over the Oregon Trail. They arrived in Cottage Grove in the 1860s. They settled southeast of town on a tributary of the Coast Fork of the Willamette River, which they named Brumbaugh River. It was later changed to Mosby Creek after David Mosby, who lived a few miles closer to town. The Brumbaughs donated land for a cemetery in the 1860s, although the first person buried there was a girl by the name of Janie Lee. The old farmhouse was built near where Mosby Creek Road and Blue Mountain School Road meet. It was later moved up the hill and remodeled. (Jones family.)

In 1850, the Donation Land Law passed. It granted 320 acres to every settler who was over 18 years old, a citizen, and a single man (or if he was married before December 1, 1851). Oregon country was the only place land was free. In other areas, land was $1.25 an acre. Settlers arriving in Oregon between 1850 and 1855 only received half as much land. (CGHS.)

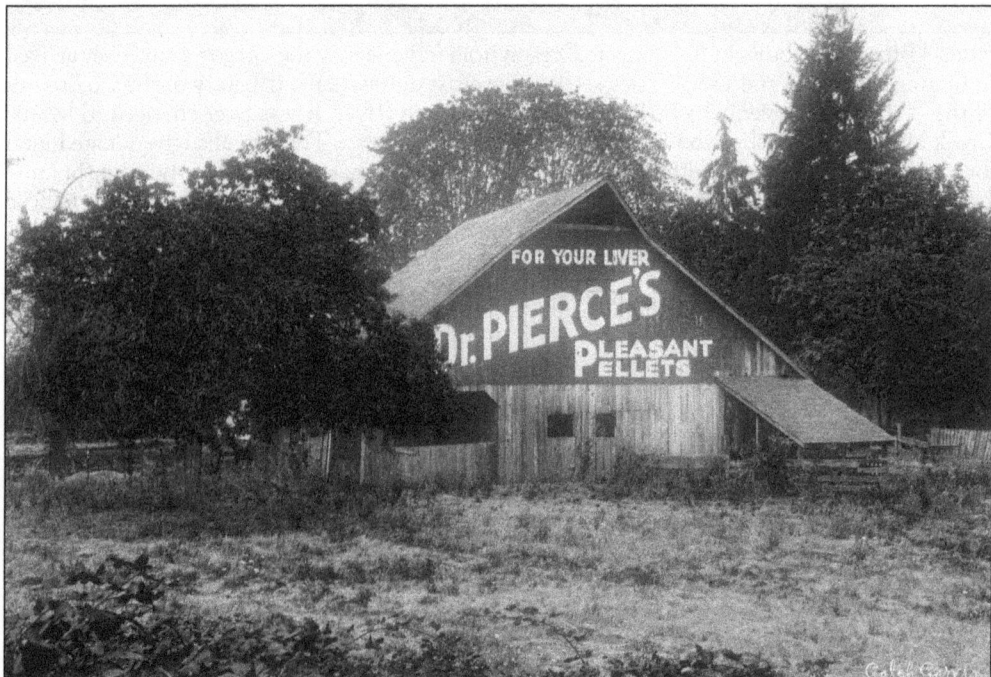

Dr. Pierce was one of the first few physicians of his era to patent the medicine he had used in his practice. After establishing a large hospital in the eastern part of the United States, he began advertising his Pleasant Pellets and his book *The Golden Medical Discovery* all over the countryside on barns, like this one in Cottage Grove. (Natural Images Photography.)

The Overholser family lived along Silk Creek. They operated three different mills consecutively from 1906 to 1954. John Overholser was the first in the family to start logging along Silk Creek, in 1909. His sons Ross, Frank, and George continued to log there until 1954. John and his wife, Nancy, also helped with running the Calapooya Springs Resort in London. They later built a house on the opposite side of the river. (CGM.)

James Chapin built his first house in what is now known as Latham in 1847. Part of the donation land claim is now partly covered by the Weyerhaeuser Company. His first house became a stopping place for those traveling up the Coast Fork Trail. He eventually built a new house with siding and glass windows. Bricks from his old house's fireplace have been found in the garden of the new home. (CGM.)

In 1850, John and James McFarland came to look at the land. They took up a land claim in 1853. James took his claim on the west side of Cochran's. John took his farther west. The McFarland claim included Mount David, named after David McFarland. The point where the McFarland claim joined the Shield claim on the south became downtown Cottage Grove's Main Street. (CGM.)

J. I. Jones was the builder of the first large-scale sawmill in the area. Booth Kelly Lumber Company purchased the Jones sawmill at Saginaw in 1898 for the sum of $70,000. J. I. Jones was elected mayor of Lemati during the feuding years between Cottage Grove and Lemati. (CGM.)

Samuel Knox and his family arrived in 1853. Knox discovered that many were being drawn to the area so he took his land claim in addition to buying more land at 50¢ an acre to make his property a total of 1,850 acres. Samuel's son Oscar Knox donated some of his land to build the Church of Christ. The oldest Knox girls rode and attended to the stock; they also married the two Veatch boys. (CGM.)

The Snapp house was built in 1894 by Dr. G. O. Snapp. A one-story structure with an unfinished attic space, its unique design included a 12-foot, 6-inch-tall spire. Dr. Snapp's medical office occupied the front of the house and living quarters for the family were in the back. (CGM.)

Alexander Cooley brought his family to Oregon from Virginia in 1853 via the Oregon Trail. He built a log cabin as his first house in Cottage Grove. As an early merchant, he located his store near the flour mill on River Road. In 1858, Alexander Cooley purchased a store near Latham from Charles Samuels. (CGM.)

Andrew Nelson put together the first electric magneto in Cottage Grove. It was located in the flour mill on River Road, the waterwheel ran the gristmill during the day and the magneto at night to provide light to a few surrounding houses. As demand grew, he upgraded the magneto and installed more poles. He sold off his business to Mountain States Power Company, which was founded in 1917. (CGHS.)

Opal Whiteley was another well-known name in Cottage Grove. Many have seen or read her diary that she started at age five. By age 13 she was giving talks on wildlife and geology. She was known for mixing nature with science and religion. When Whiteley reached 21, she had written her first book, and while trying to get it published, her diary was chosen instead. By then, Whiteley had begun to tell people that she was a lost princess from France sent to live in Oregon to be protected from kidnappers. She insisted she was not a Whiteley and was only raised by them. (CGHS.)

In 1852, David Mosby took his claim east of Mosby Creek. Just as the other local families, Dave Mosby made his cash from his hogs. He would butcher as many as 60 in a year and pack the meat in a saltbox he made by hewing out the center of a 30-inch log. After a few days in the salt, the ham, shoulders, and side of bacon were hung from poles wall to wall in the smokehouse. To cure the meat, a slow fire of vine maple was kept smoldering and smoking. When the meat was ready, it was sold in Portland, and on his return, he would bring back his supplies. (Above, CGHS; below, CGM.)

The Veatch family was large and well liked in the town. This is evident in many of their family photographs, like the one below of the picnic at the Veatchs' place held during an outing to cut wood for the Presbyterian church. The Veatch's 50th wedding anniversary party, above, is another example of their extensive group of friends and family. Pictured from left to right are (first row) Millard McGee Mosby, Harvey Scott Holderman, Joseph Veatch McGee, Veta Veatch Holderman, Robert Harvey Mosby, Rosetta Blanch McGee, Rosetta Dove McGee, Samuel Russel Veatch, and George Small Mosby; (second row) Oliver O, Lucinda Jane Christman Veatch, child Evalyn Claire Veatch, Mary Suphening Veatch Mosby, child Darrel Knox Mosby, Harvey Clayburn Veatch, Robert Elhanon Veatch, Margaret Knox Veatch, Eva Jane Veatch Holderman, child Dorris George Holderman, Mabel Preston Veatch, Willie Ruth McGee, Lillian Elizebeth Veatch, and David Clayburn Mosby. (CGM.)

W. E. Edwards and his bride, Lorena McFarland, built a new house on Chestnut Street in the late 1800s. It was built with wide porches for drying clothes in the winter and shade in the summer. Boardwalks were built throughout most of the growing city allowing children a place to play out of the muddy streets. Ramps were constructed at the street crossings to allow horse-drawn vehicles to cross the boardwalks. (CGM.)

Soon after Oregon became a state, the United States was embroiled in the Civil War. Very few Cottage Grove men went east to fight, but numerous Civil War veterans came to Oregon shortly after the war ended. In this picture, Civil War veterans gather at the Cottage Grove cemetery. (CGM.)

Four

EARLY SCHOOLS
AND CHURCHES

The first school operating in the city limits started in 1879; classes were held in the Union Church. The first teacher was Oscar Knox. In 1880, a new school was constructed. It consisted of two floors and was located on the corner of Second Street and Adams Street.

The Doolittle's homestead was located on Cerro-Gordo about 6 miles east of Cottage Grove. The Crites-Doolittle School was located on the homestead. The schoolhouse was built about 1904. The Doolittle's children, along with some children from nearby homesteads, attended the school, which was warmed by a small fireplace in the center of the room. The school closed its doors in 1917. (CGHS.)

The second schoolhouse in the Cottage Grove area was the Knox School. The land for the school was donated by Samuel Knox and the school was built next to the Row River. The schoolhouse was often called the Row River School. Opened in 1865, it was a wooden one-room schoolhouse located several miles northeast of the earlier Currin Schoolhouse. Teachers in the school were Rufus Callison, Minerva Knox, and Oscar Knox. (CGM.)

David McFarland divided his spare land on the west side of his claim into smaller parcels. He sold most of the pieces off to families for their homes, but one parcel he donated to the Catholics, who then erected their little white church. The Catholic church was eventually turned into the Cottage Grove Museum. (CGM.)

The West Side School was constructed in 1904 to serve as a grade school for all the children living on the western side of the Coast Fork. The school was three-stories tall with a daylight basement. Latham School used the West Side School while theirs was being remodeled in 1940. It was torn down before 1950 to make way for the Cottage Grove Hospital, which opened in 1951. (CGM.)

Clay Mosby sits second from the left in the second row. This was the eighth-grade class of 1904–1905. The eighth-grade classes were located on the second floor of the West Side School. Between 1905 and 1907, the principal of the school was Chambers Strange. The eighth-grade teacher was Worth Harvey. From 1905 until 1907, one hundred percent of the eighth-grade students passed the state examinations. (CGM.)

In 1913, work began on the Cottage Grove High School. A ceremony was held and the cornerstone of the building was placed as many locals looked on with excitement. The school originally was the Cottage Grove High School but later became the Jefferson Elementary School. (CGHS.)

The first high school built within Cottage Grove's city limits was erected in 1892. The wooden-frame schoolhouse was located at Jefferson and Adams Streets. The high school was on the second floor, and the lower grades were on the first floor. The first class graduated in 1896. (CGM.)

The children from the Dorena area would walk to Culp Creek to attend school. In 1903, the Dorena Schoolhouse was built just above the present-day school and called the "Star Schoolhouse." The main building housed the school bell along with the grade school, and the high school classes were held in a second structure just to the right of the schoolhouse. (CGHS.)

Between 1914 and 1915, the teachers of Dorena High School were Almeda Dean, Esther Anderson, Ella Anderson, and K. K. Robinson. The last class graduated from Dorena High School in 1936. The teacher was L. W. Fortner, and his graduating class included Robert Wagner, Robert Vaughn, and Mary Doolittle. Ten years later, the schoolhouse was torn down to make way for the Dorena Dam, and a new one was built above the dam. (CGHS.)

The Carpus Prairie School was established in 1865 in the community of Hebron. It was in use until 1883 when the Hebron School was constructed. The Hebron School served many students for over 53 years, from 1883 to 1940. The schoolhouse had one room for all eight grades until 1927 when the schoolhouse was divided into two rooms and hired a second teacher. (CGM.)

Wildwood Schoolhouse was opened in 1884 and closed in 1940. It was located on Row River Road near the Wildwood Falls, just a little ways away from the Red Covered Bridge. Many of the miners had brought their families with them, and as towns boomed on the route to the mines, more schools soon became necessary. (CGM.)

Henry Small donated the southern corner of his land claim for the site of the schoolhouse. As this was the first one built in the Coast Fork Valley, he picked the site carefully. The original building was believed to have been of log construction. Henry may have known it was going to be the earliest school built, but it would probably come as a surprise if someone had told him back then that his school would continue to operate for well over 150 years. Latham School has always had a family atmosphere with classroom picnics and get-togethers. (CGHS.)

School was first held at the Silk Creek Schoolhouse in 1878. It was the only school in the 12 miles between Lorane and Cottage Grove. The oldest official record shows Elizabeth Hutchinson as the teacher in 1905. In a time before busses, it was a long walk to school for the children living on the west side of Cottage Grove. In 1910, Curtis Veatch and Wilber McFarland were able to form Cedars, a new district which was 4 miles east of Silk Creek. On many a warm day one could find the children enjoying a picnic lunch on the banks of Silk Creek. (CGHS.)

Walden School was a log cabin schoolhouse that started its first class sometime around 1862. The schoolhouse was known to locals as Walden School, but at one point in time was also known as the Shields and Walker Schoolhouse. The first known teacher was Nancy Small (David Mosby's sister) and for the second term it was Green Davis. (CGHS.)

The one-room schoolhouse had several children attending classes at once; it ran from first grade through sixth grade. One well-known student at Walden School was Opal Whitely. She is photographed here in a 1907 class photograph. Several of the students would have had to light their ways with coal oil lanterns while walking to school at 6:00 in the morning. (CGHS.)

The first London School was built in 1895. Settlers were drawn by the Mineral Springs Resort and logging in the area. By 1910, with enrollment up to 40 students, the town decided to build a new two-room schoolhouse, purchasing land from W. W. Shortridge. Construction started after the close of the 1912 fall term. (CGHS.)

Located at London crossroads, the London Church of Christ was built by John Sutherland Sr. and W. T. Jones in 1889. It is the oldest Church of Christ in Oregon and the only church in the community of London. It is still in use to this day and is one of the few remaining churches with a bell in the belfry. (CGHS.)

On January 16, 1860, the 31st school district paid John W. and Rebecca A. Richardson $3 for 1 acre located next to the Brumbaugh River (today's Mosby Creek). The one-room schoolhouse was completed in the late 1870s. Many early homesteaders sent their children to attend school at what is known as Blue Mountain School. These settlers included John Allen, William Spong, George Downes, Billy Griggs, George Lowry, Jack Brumbaugh, John Palmer, the Licketys, and the Millers. In 1913, a one-room addition was built to house the high school. School officials purchased the best laboratory equipment and typewriters; the school's budget included substantial state timber tax money paid by Booth Kelly Lumber Company. All funds had to be spent each year and any remainder returned to the state. This meant that the rural school had whatever, whenever. (CGHS.)

The First Baptist Church originally held its Sunday school in a passenger train car until the church was finished in 1925. When it was finished, its building had not only one but two auditoriums. Its design was somewhat of a Spanish mission style with plastered walls inside and stucco outside walls along with stained-glass windows in the front. When it was finally finished, it would be the most ostentatious church in town. (CGHS.)

This is the Bible class of 1919. Pictured from left to right are (first row) Mrs. White, Mrs. Wilkenson, Mrs. Abel, and Lillie Longfellow; (second row) Mrs. Arne, Mrs. Ralston, Mrs. Porter, and four unidentified; (third row) James Longfellow, Mr. Wilkerson, Lois Woolley, Anna Hubbell, Laura Woolley, and two unidentified; (fourth row) Jim Benson, Ike Jones, Dr. McCargan, and two unidentified. The teachers on the right are Mr. and Mrs. Simbral. (CGHS.)

Punishments

	Lashes
1. Boys and Girls Playing Together	4
2. Fighting at School	5
3. Quareling at School	5
4. Gambleing or Betting at School	4
5. Playing at Cards at School	10
6. Climbing for Every Foot Over Three Feet Up a Tree	1
7. Telling Lies	7
8. Telling Tales Out of School	8
9. Giving Each Other Ill Names	3
10. Swaring at School	8
11. For Misbehaving to Girls	10
12. For Drinking Spiritous Liquors at School	8
13. Making Swings and Swinging on Them	7
14. For Waring Long Finger Nails	2
15. Misbehaving to Persons on the Road	4
16. For Going to Girls Play Places	3
17. Girls Going to Boys Play Places	3
18. Coming to School With Dirty Faces and Hands	2
19. For Calling Each Other Liars	4
20. For Wrestling at School	4
21. For Weting Each Other Washing at Playtime	2
22. Scuffling at School	4
23. For Going and Playing about the Mill or Creek	6
24. For Going about the Barn or doing any Mischief about the Place	7

10 November 1818

School rules in the 1800s were different than they are today, but more than anything, the punishment was worse. One could receive four lashes from the teacher for calling someone a liar, seven lashes for making swings and swinging on them, or 10 lashes for playing cards at school. Today's after-school detention seems mild punishment in comparison. (CGHS.)

Five

MOUNTAIN OF MINES

In 1866, the miners established a Code of Laws that set up boundaries and created several rules that they were all to follow. The laws covered things like the sizes of land claims. The article stated a claim had to be a set size of 100 by 25 yards. It also limited the number of claims to one per person and two to the original locator, set the size of town lots at 50 by 75 feet, and insisted a house or fence be built on the lot if the land was to be held. (BMM.)

Bohemia City thrived during the mining boom. Miners' cabins spotted the hillside and smoke from the sawmill promised lumber for more houses, railroad ties, and the mines. There were many men that lived at the mines with their families all winter long. The logs also provided warmth for the families. (BMM.)

The small sawmill at the Champion Mine was one of the first things to be built at Bohemia. Getting the boiler and steam engine up the mountain to the mill was quite a feat at the time. The roads were little more than trails through the forest that ended with a sharp grade up the mountainside. (BMM.)

The tram was also a popular way to get from the bottom of the hill to the top without exerting any effort. Margie Knowles is riding the tramway from the Musick Mine to the Champion Mine. Notice the telephone lines on the side enabling instant communication from one end to the other. (BMM.)

Once an outcropping of ore was located, miners tunneled into the mountain, following the vein to extract the easy milling oxidized ore. In 1905, high-grade ore was hit in the Champion Mine. The pocket was so rich that only trusted miners were allowed in the tunnel. Canvas was laid out on the floor and the walls were bushed down onto it. One miner said the walls glittered like a jewelry store. (BMM.)

George McQueen, James Plaster, and James Potts were drivers for the Bohemia Stage. The stage offered service between Cottage Grove and the Mineral Hotel, which was located at the base of Hardscrabble Road. It was a two-day ride from Cottage Grove to the Mineral Hotel, so most people spent the night wanting to be well rested before tackling the treacherous daylong climb to Bohemia City. One miner, known as Bohemia Smithy, started the trip to Bohemia City with a jug of whiskey one evening and after failing to arrive when expected, a search party was sent out. He was found hanging in a small fir tree off the side of a cliff, singing, his jug in hand, just waiting to be rescued after he had stumbled off the cliff in the dark. (Above, CGM; below, BMM.)

The stamp mill at the Champion Mine consisted of 10 stamps. The ore dropped in the top chute, went through the jaw crusher, and was then sifted into the stamps. A screen kept the ore under the stamps until it was pulverized. A stream of water washed the fines out onto a concentrating table covered with mercury. As the water washed over the table, the heavy gold dropped into the mercury. After a run, the mercury was scraped from the table and processed. (CGM.)

The stamp mill was a vital piece of equipment at the mines. Without it, the ore would have to be carried out to another mill. The stamp mills were manufactured by Hammond Manufacturing Company in Portland, Oregon. After being freighted to Cottage Grove, they were disassembled into pieces small enough to fit on a mule. They were reassembled at the mines and put into use immediately. (BMM.)

New gold strikes always drew a crowd. Often, miners disappointed with the diggings at one site would pull up and move as soon as the next big strike was made. Not many made it big and most of the claims were bought out by few companies. A large hotel was built at the Champion Mine to house incoming miners and their families. (BMM.)

A pair of miners, conserving their energy, rode the tram from the mill to the mine where the real work would begin. The mine was located about 1,000 feet higher than the mill. This gave the mill easy access to firewood and ample water supplies that were not available at the higher elevations. (BMM.)

Robert Mosby and Jim Cole were the first men to take machinery by packhorse to the mine by way of the Knott Trail. They used two horses, one in front of the other, a few feet apart. They equipped them with a metal U that had a hook on each end to go over a horse pack and saddle. A pole was placed in the hooks on each side of the horse and the machinery was on the poles in the middle. (BMM.)

Wagon trains were common to see on the trails to the mines. The tolls of the Bohemia Wagon Road for June 3, 1893, to April 1, 1894, were as such: "Each wagon and buggies with one horse or one mule was 75¢, each man and horse 50¢, each pack animal 25¢, each loose horse or cattle 10¢, and each sheep, hog, or goat 5¢." (BMM.)

Bohemia City was the first settlement to be established in the Bohemia Mountains. It was located on the Musick Mine site. In 1868, John Alexander and Bird Farrier built a number of cabins and several buildings at Bohemia City, and in 1868, a road was built to the area. (BMM.)

In 1895, a roll of wire cable one and three-quarter miles long and weighing in at over 7,000 pounds was freighted to the Champion Mine. It was used to run a tramline from the mine down to the mill that was located at 4,500 feet of elevation. The mill was built much lower on the mountain to provide a constant source of water and wood as well as a warmer climate. (BMM.)

As the mining area grew, so did the need for more equipment to be brought up the mountain by pack train. The trails to the mines were so narrow and windy that occasionally passing areas were made. To help with this, L. C. Scott introduced the idea of putting freight bells on the lead teams to let people know that another wagon was coming and to wait in the turnout. (BMM.)

The Bohemia Hotel and post office provided accommodations for some of the 400 miners that worked the mines there, as well as mail service to the outside world. Note that some of the siding is made from leftover crate sides. The man on the far right is in the process of disassembling the remaining crates for more siding. (BMM.)

The first winter that supplies were freighted into Bohemia City was in 1934. During the winter, freight was hauled by truck to the snow line, where it was transferred to a sled and then hauled by a tractor the rest of the way. Much of the mining was done during the winter. The men would pack the dynamite they used for blasting in their boot tops to keep it from freezing. (CGM.)

The office of the Champion Mine is pictured here. First from left is Alex Lundberg. The fourth from the left is Elizabeth Lundberg. They were the mail carriers for the Bohemia mining district where mail was delivered two or three times a week. Usually, it was delivered early enough in the day that one could read the mail and write a reply to be sent out the following morning. (BMM.)

76

Horses were an expense some could not afford, and miners surely needed a wheelbarrow anyway, so these two decided to hoof it to the mines. It is hard to imagine pushing a wheelbarrow full of tools 40 miles into the mountains. Thankfully, one man could push while the other helped by pulling on the rope.

Below, a tramway was built to move gold ore from the mines down to the stamp mill for processing. A one-and-three-quarter-miles-long cable was freighted to the mine in 1895 and used to pull the ore carts to and from the mine. This made the process of transporting the ore to the mill much easier. (BMM.)

After new owners from back east bought out the Noonday mining claims, they built a new tramway and 20 stamp mills. Unfortunately, they did not do a thorough assay and ran into sulphide ore just a few feet into the shaft. All the hard work on the new construction was for naught. (CGM.)

The LeRoy and Purvance children were working out some excess energy on the new Noonday mining tramway. This was taken during the summer of 1915. These children did not receive a summer vacation, and instead spent the time helping out their fathers at the mines. Most of the big mines had trams, providing rides up and down the mountain over the active mining areas. (CGM.)

The Painted Post Ranch was the first overnight stopping point for the stage service to the mines. A wagon road was completed from Culp Creek to the ranch in 1895. Accommodations, food, and fresh horses were kept for the stage service at the Painted Post and at Mineral Hotel, the stopping point for the second night of the three-day-long stage trip. (BMM.)

The stage at the Painted Post Ranch, after the wagon road was completed to the mines in 1905, made travel to and from the mines much easier. The wagons often carried machinery and foodstuffs to the mines and 100-pound sacks of ore concentrates and even the occasional gold brick back into town. (BMM.)

The Vesuvius Mine was located on the western side of Fairview Mountain. At first, the Vesuvius did not have its own mill. Its ore was sent to the Stocks and Harlow Mill for processing. The Graber brothers took over the mine and moved the old mill from the Knott claim to the Vesuvius. A stamp mill was erected after the property sold to F. J. Hard in 1902. (CGHS.)

S. P. Garoutte discovered an outcrop of cinnabar on Black Butte in 1897 after a landslide. W. B. Dennis bought the property in 1898 and just a year later made his first shipment of 2,700 pounds of mercury to New York. Five miles of tunnels were opened and 40 veins of ore were located in the first 10 years of operation. (BMM.)

This shows the reduction plant at the Black Butte Mercury Mine. Cinnabar ore was blasted from the mine and hauled down to the processing plant. The ore was crushed and heated to 1,200 degrees, vaporizing the mercury. The vapors then passed through a cooling tower that condensed the mercury vapors into what is now known as quicksilver. (BMM.)

The main tunnel entrance to the Black Butte Mine is located at 1,000 feet of elevation. In 1927, the mine owner expanded operations to Dennis Creek a short distance away. After excavating 2,000 feet of tunnel into the mountain, they ran into a large lime deposit, and so for a few years the Black Butte Mine also produced agricultural lime and screened lime used for poultry grit. (BMM.)

The Oregon chamber in the Black Butte Mine is pictured here in 1922. A short line named the Peavine and Western was built from the reduction plant to the mine in 1927. The tiny train consisted of a gas engine manufactured by the Milwaukee Iron Works, five side-dump ore cars, and a flat car used to haul tools and dynamite to the mine. At its peak, the mine produced 100 tons of mercury ore a day. It is still considered to be one of the richest mercury mines in the history of the United States. London Springs' guesthouses and mineral spring fountain were located just down the hill from the plant. (BMM.)

Six

CALAPOOYA SPRINGS

The hotel was known to be a riot of activity during Fourth of July celebrations. Wild West rodeos that were organized by Guy and Willie Ray and their cowboys drew thousands of spectators. The locals even joined together and started a band, which played on the hotel's front lawn during the celebration. (CGHS.)

Calapooya Mineral Springs Hotel was built by Levi Geer in the 1900s. It was located about 12 miles southeast of Cottage Grove. The area is known to locals as the London District. People from

miles around came to bathe in the magical waters of the "healing mineral springs." (CGHS.)

Calapooya Springs added a slide to the bathhouse in 1925. This was a huge hit with all the visitors. Water was piped from the springs near the riverbank, just east of the hotel, to the bathhouse. The bathhouse was a two-story building with many individual rooms. The upper floor was occupied by the baths and on the first floor was the large swimming tank made from cedar timbers. The adults swam in the deep end and the children had a shallow wading area to play in. There was a large steam boiler at the end of the pool that piped hot water into a large storage tank feeding the pool and baths. (CGHS.)

In addition to the mineral baths at Calapooya Springs Resort, one could also enjoy the many different activities. Often games of tennis and croquet were held on the lawns along with horse races and motorcycle races that everyone would watch. (CGHS.)

The Fourth of July celebration of the Calapooya Mineral Springs Hotel was an all-day event—of course a good part of that was the 12-mile-long trip by wagon. They offered a live band, sumptuous dining, a fireworks display, as well as horse and motorcycle races. The Wild West Rodeo was brought in yearly by Guy and Willie Ray and drew thousands. After the festivities, cooling off in the pool and the waterslide were quite popular. (CGHS.)

Calapooya Springs London Oregon

The water from the Calapooya Mineral Springs at one time had been shipped out to many parts of the county. A huge bottling works was built, and the mineral water was bottled and also made into soda pop and sold throughout the United States. The bottled mineral water and soda pop became so popular that it was even shipped to England and used in drinks that were served at bars. The first bottling plant was built over the swamp west of the bathhouse. Later a larger two-story building was constructed on the banks of the Coast Fork River just across from the Calapooya Springs Hotel. The upstairs of the large bottling plant was used for London's community activities, parties, and dances. Many said the mineral water tasted like rotten eggs. (CGHS.)

Bottling Works Calapooya Mineral Springs London Oregon

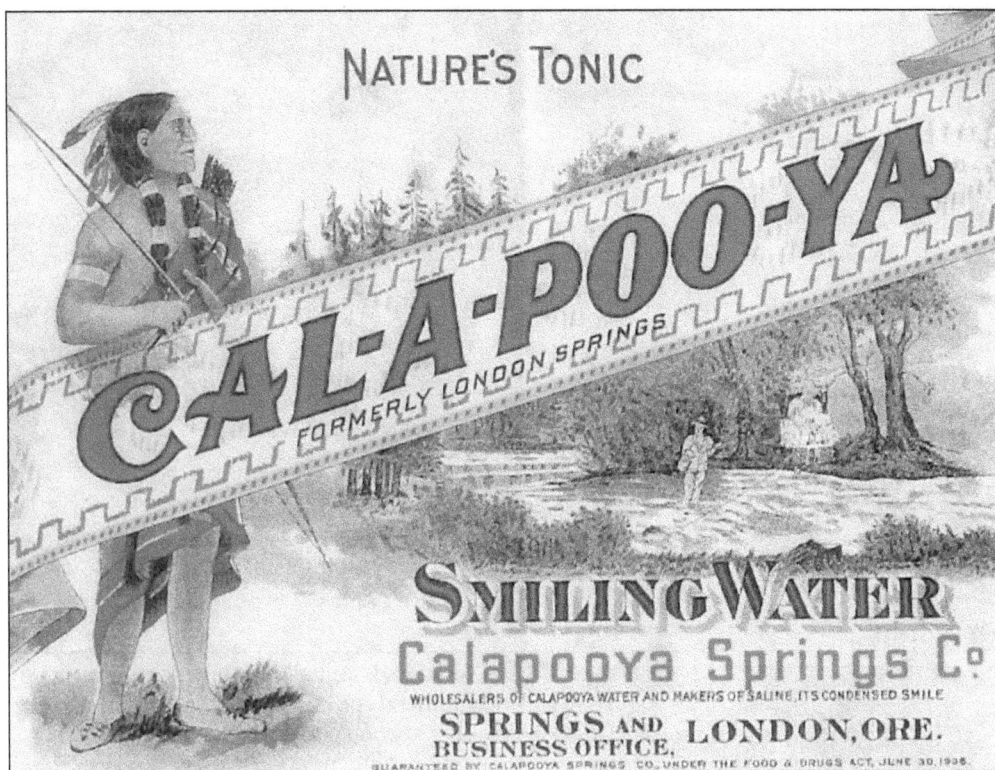

NATURE'S TONIC

CAL·A·POO·YA

FORMERLY LONDON SPRINGS

SMILING WATER

Calapooya Springs Co.

WHOLESALERS OF CALAPOOYA WATER AND MAKERS OF SALINE, ITS CONDENSED SMILE

SPRINGS AND BUSINESS OFFICE. LONDON, ORE.

GUARANTEED BY CALAPOOYA SPRINGS CO. UNDER THE FOOD & DRUGS ACT, JUNE 30, 1936.

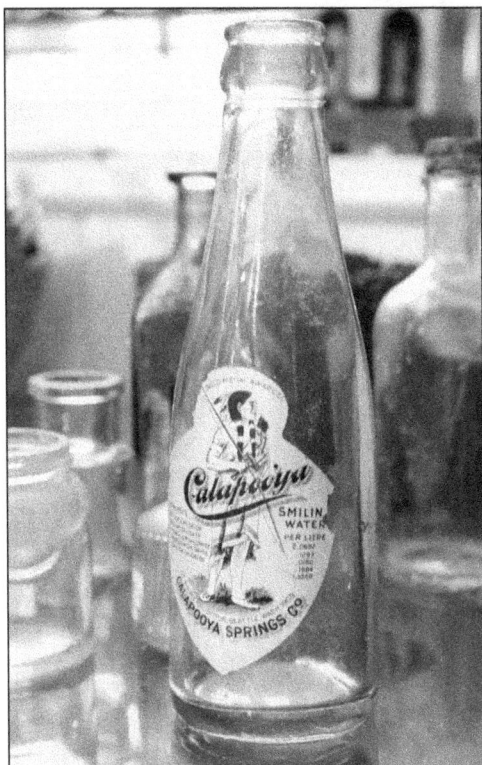

Calapooya Springs Company used a colorful label showing a Native American in full ceremonial dress (regalia). After the bottles received their label, they were then boxed in wooden crates, and hauled with horses and wagons to the train station in Cottage Grove. It was rumored that "one day, while on its way to the railroad station a wagon load of soda pop crates fell over, a few nice teenage boys helped pick up and reload the wagon, later to be discovered the wagon was one soda pop case lighter." It is said that that afternoon the boys drank to their health. (Above, CGHS; right, Natural Images Photography.)

A small rock well was built at the point where the mineral springs emerged on the riverbank so that anyone passing by could sample the famous healing mineral waters. A raised white bridge crossed the river and allowed people to go from the resort across to the London Store for mail and groceries. (CGM.)

Bernice Berggren took a break on the riverbank at London Springs Resort. In order to save money on pipe, John Overholser came up with a way to drill 3-inch holes through 10-foot-long fir poles. He then connected them with short pieces of iron pipe. This supplied water for some 1,500 feet from the river to the resort. (CGHS.)

Not far from the Calapooya Springs Resort was the London Store founded by John Sutherland. At the store, one could find all the groceries for a picnic, local gossip, and their mail. Locals and guests could cross over the creek on a little, white bridge. They would find themselves walking among tall trees into an inviting park with a playground and picnic tables. (CGHS.)

When the Calapooya Mineral Springs Resort became popular, the London area began to boom. The school built in 1895 was no longer big enough. Attendance was up to 28 students in 1909 and by 1910 was up to 40. Payment of $125 was made to W. W. Ashortridge for additional land. The school was enlarged to two rooms and construction was finished in time for the 1912 spring term. (CGHS.)

The Massey family poses for the camera on their front porch at their house in London in 1909. Mary Massey was a cousin of Anna Ogelsby. The Massey's were active in the Coast Fork Grange No. 243, organized in 1890, which met in a hall near Wilson Creek until a Grange was organized in London in 1954. (CGM.)

Amos Sutherland had the first store and post office in London, which was originally called Amos, named after John Amos Sutherland Jr., the son of the postmaster. In 1903, the new London Store and post office was built and the name was changed to London because of the confusion over the similar sounding town of Ames, Oregon. (CGHS.)

Seven

LOGGING SAVES THE DAY

Logging began in Cottage Grove in early 1867 when William Whitney built a sawmill on his land claim in the east side of the Hebron Valley. Logging in 1895 would have been a challenge, but this did not stop the men of Cottage Grove. It was quite the sight to see the horses pulling their loads to the mill. (CGM.)

In 1907, loggers used locomotives at every opportunity. Narrow winding tracks were laid on forest paths around stumps and boulders using such hastily constructed trestles to cross ravines that the engineer and fireman would not ride the train across them. Instead, they set the engine dead slow and walked across. After the timber within reach had been harvested, the tracks were dismantled and hauled to the next site. (CGM.)

After the invention of the steam donkey and wire rope, the spar pole was soon to follow. It allowed the donkey to pull logs from across a hill using a skyline. A boom arm was made from a couple of logs and gave the crew the ability to easily sort and stack the logs as they were piled up on the landing. (CGM.)

Brown Lumber Company was owned by Willis E. Brown. He arrived in Row County to create a mill at Dorena in 1902. The Brown Lumber Company logged at Nesmith in 1910, at Rocky Point in 1913, and at Rujada in 1915. The lumber company used a short line with the "Shay" locomotive to haul their logs out of the mountain areas to Disston. (CGM.)

Brown Lumber Company, below, was located near the railroad tracks because all the lumber mills transported their logs from the mountains to the lumber mills. The tall stack on the left belongs to the electric light plant. The center stacks in the photograph belong to Brown's company. The Cottage Grove Cannery is in the distance to the right. (CGHS.)

The defunct Stocks and Harlow Mill was bought up by the newly formed Bohemia Lumber Company in 1917. Jack McGladry was in charge of getting the mill up and running again. After almost a month, the mill was sawing lumber. That very night, on August 27, the Brown Mill in Cottage Grove burned to the ground and with it a million board feet of finished lumber. (CGHS.)

Loggers often were sent out to tackle large trees in the old growth forest with nothing but their own strength. They would cut a notch into a tree and then place a springboard in it to raise themselves above the butt swell and the pitch seams of the trees. With a two-man crew they would use a large handsaw to cut through the tree. (CGM.)

The Disston Post Office was established in 1906 and ran until 1974. Cranston Jones, the first postmaster, was also one of the founders of the first sawmill in Disston, and the name of the town came from the famous Disston saw. At one time, there were two sawmills in Disston, the Wheeler-Osgood Lumber Company and the I. E. James Lumber Company. (CGHS.)

It has been stated that in 1909 there was 31 mills in operation using Cottage Grove as their home base. The monthly payroll was in excess of $50,000. Jones Sawmill at Disston was one of the 31 mills. This photograph of the 1911 crew consisted of 20 to 30 men with Alfred Whiteman top center. (CGM.)

The crew of the Durable Fir Lumber Company resided in the Row River Valley at the foot of Cerro Gordo. The site currently lies at the bottom of Dorena Lake. Operations shut down in 1949 as the dam neared completion. The buildings were moved or dismantled before the reservoir began to fill in 1950. The lumberyard served the town as well as the mines upriver. To the right of the church, along old Row River Road, were the post office and school as well as the store of Scott Chrisman, who also worked as a freighter hauling goods to the mines. (CGHS.)

Many of the lumber and mining towns had a breakfast house for the workers. The Booth-Kelly camp was no different than any other. The sign over the front door let everyone know that breakfast was served every morning at 6:10 a.m. and the kitchen doors closed everyday at 20 minutes to 7:00 p.m. on the dot. (CGM.)

John Kelly, Jack McGladry, and George Kelly went into a partnership to form the Mohawk Lumber Company, located at Donna in the Mohawk Valley, just east of Springfield. Over the next couple years, the venture became very profitable. David and Carrol Auld, investment bankers from Kansas, were determined to buy it. After much dickering, the Aulds accepted the terms set forth by the partners. (CGM.)

In 1899, Booth-Kelly Lumber Company's millpond and ramshackle camp house at Prune Hill, near Saginaw, typified small lumber operations of the day. The company would become the lumber industry's largest player in the region around Cottage Grove. (CGM.)

Pond soaking made logs easier to mill and less prone to splitting. This millpond was located up Mosby Creek and was used as a storage and sorting yard. It was equipped with a boom used to set the logs onto railcars for the short trip north on the Oregon Pacific and Eastern Railway (OP&E) to the sawmill. (CGHS.)

The Booth-Kelly crew and a small steam yarder, the first steam donkey, went to work in 1881. Envisioned by John Dolbeer, who took a dockside winch used to unload ships and mounted it on skids, it could pull itself from site to site gathering massive piles of logs in a short time. (CGM.)

Sawyer Jack McGladry sits astraddle the log as he and the crew pause operations and pose for a picture. Known as "Black Jack" for his temper, he was never one to walk away from a fight. In one brawl, when he was getting the upper hand, his assailant pulled a derringer and shot Jack in the mouth, knocking him to the floor. After sitting up, he spat out the bullet. (CGM.)

A massive ice storm in January 1909 enveloped the Booth-Kelly flume with ice. After boards were rough sawn, they traveled the 6 miles down the flume to the planer mill at Saginaw. At full capacity, nine railcars of lumber traveled the flume each day. Workers stood on catwalks up to 110 feet in the air and cleared out lumber jams and plugging leaks. (CGM.)

Booth-Kelly Lumber Company acquired the holdings of J. I. Jones, which were located on Prune Hill, in 1895 for $70,000. There, they built what was said to be a primitive camp with a large operation. The lumber company also began to harvest timber off Row River Mill at Culp Creek in 1949. (CGHS.)

At the first Bohemia Lumber Company mill, in the Row River area east of Cottage Grove, LaSells Stewart (right) was the head sawyer. The time was 1917, and the mill used old-growth timber to manufacture railroad ties and lumber. Bohemia eventually became one of the largest wood products companies in the world. (CGM.)

The No. 2 engine operated by J. H. Chambers hauled logs from the surrounding hillsides into the mill and shuttled railcars of finished lumber to the switchyard to the north. In 1917, Chambers bought out the OP&E for a mere $53,750—a fifth of its estimated value just four years earlier. (CGHS.)

The first J. H. Chambers Sawmill was built during the early 1900s; it was located a few miles south of Cottage Grove. Chambers also established a mill at Dorena a few miles east of Cottage Grove. By 1909, the mills had a capacity of 40,000 board feet of lumber per day. Within 10 years,

Chambers was producing 70,000 board feet of lumber a day. In 1925, the covered railroad bridge bearing his name was built on the west side of the mill and with it, the short line towards Lorane opened up access to the vast timber stands to the west of Cottage Grove. (CGM.)

The J. H. Chambers and Son Sawmill crew are shown here in 1914 at a mill below Latham and upriver from the later mill sites with the covered bridge. The circular saw blades of the valley's many mills churned out excessive sawdust. Unique among the industries of the time, the waste product of the steam-powered sawmill was used to fuel the boilers. (CGM.)

The steam donkey revolutionized logging in the 1880s with its abundance of horsepower, multiple cable winches, and the ability to literally tow itself to the job site. Before the arrival of the steam donkey, ox teams with single-bitted axes and chains, or horse teams, were the only way around the mountains. (CGHS.)

A large dam was built across the Willamette River near the J. H. Chambers and Son Sawmill in the Latham area. It was used to divert water into the millrace that powered the flour mills and the electric plant. The millrace was filled in after the last flour mill burned, although the concrete footings for the dam on the banks of the river remain to this day. (CGM.)

Every winter River Road flooded, so when the Chambers railroad bridge was built above high water, they had to build a ramp to enable traffic to cross the tracks. This truck carrying spare axles for the train was overweight, causing the ramp to collapse. A crane was brought in to help clean up the mess. (CGHS.)

Fire could sweep through the sawmill in a few hours. Bucket brigades were able to form quickly and put out the fire, if caught early. The Chambers Mill caught fire many times throughout the years. One of the biggest fires was in the late 1900s. It not only burned the mill to the ground, but 5 million board feet of lumber also went up in smoke. Lumber is measured by board foot. This cubic measurement is the result of multiplying the length, width, and height of a piece of stock. One board foot is equal to 12 inches square by 1 inch thick or 144 cubic inches. That single fire was reported to have cost the mill $250,000 in addition to many months of lost production. (CGM.)

Many of the slopes were too steep for locomotives, so the loggers would use steam donkeys. They would hook the cable to the railcars and winch them up and down the mountainside. This method enabled the logging crews to push even deeper into the canyons and higher up the mountainsides. (CGHS.)

Virgil D. White and John Coffman pause for a quick moment in the limelight while working in the boiler room at the J. H. Chambers and Son Sawmill. The steam-powered sawmill was one of few self-sustaining industries around. The sawmill actually produced much more sawdust than the mill required to fire the boilers, so the rest was sent over to the wigwam burner. (CGM.)

Early drag saws were usually powered by oxen or mules pulling a gear-drive mechanism in a circle. The gearbox pulled the saw back and forth. In later years, small engines were harnessed to the drag saw, enabling crews to saw much more quickly. The trusty drag saw cut a good amount of firewood in the days before chainsaws. (CGHS.)

When the Booth-Kelly crew was logging on prune hill, the loggers lived in camps. Some lived in tents with wooden floors, others lived in small houses that were built on skids and would be dragged from site to site. When they ran out of logs, they simply moved the camp. For a quick ride to town, they would hop on a piece of lumber and ride the flume to the planer mill. (CGM.)

110

In 1917, A. L. Woodard's mill was built and later sold to Woodard's son, Walter A. Woodard. A flume was built from that mill to the Hebron district to carry the rough lumber from the sawmill to the finishing plant at Latham. Woodard built a second sawmill on the west side of the valley in the Hebron district. The original mill in the London district was known as "Camp A." The Hebron mill was called "Camp B." (CGM.)

The section crew laid temporary railroad tracks into new stands of timber. After they finished, the loggers would move in and harvest the trees. Donkeys pulled the railcars up steep grades and slowly lowered them back down loaded with logs. When all the logs were hauled to the mill, the section crew would pull up the tracks and lay them to a new stand of trees. (CGM.)

River Rats, as they were called, earned about $3 a day, which was twice as much as the going wage. They would ride the logs downstream, driving them with poles and peaveys. If the logs got caught in the rocks or brush it would cause a logjam. The River Rats would then have to pry the logs loose or cut them free to get the raft moving again. The River Rats wore spiked boots to ensure a good grip on the slippery logs; they had to have a great sense of balance or they did not last long. (CGM.)

Eight

RIDING THE RAILS

The Brown Lumber Company hauled logs with train engine No. 9, also known to locals as the "Shay." The train ran between the logging yard and the logging sites in Nesmith, Rocky Point, Rujada, and Disston in the early 1900s. The Shay was a gear locomotive instead of a piston power, which gave it the ability to haul heavier loads up the steeper grades and also enabled it to go around sharper corners. (MGC.)

The railroad station in town was painted yellow with a large sign with black lettering that read, "Cottage Grove, 144 mi. to Portland and 53 mi. to Roseburg." The railroad depot had three rooms: the baggage room, the office with a telegraph machine, and the waiting room. The waiting room was furnished with a large black coal stove situated in the center of the room. It was not too uncommon to find Green Pitcher, the city policeman, and Frank McFarland, the night cop, huddled around the stove to keep warm on many winter days. (Above, CGM; below, CGHS.)

The old Oregon Central made her maiden voyage down the east side of the Coast Fork on July 7, 1872. When a train approached town, everybody rushed out to greet it. Once, when a passenger asked about the population of the town, the conductor replied, "Just wait and you will see everyone in Cottage Grove at the depot." This day in 1911, William Howard Taft was campaigning for the presidency. (CGM.)

The dispatch office was responsible for setting the train schedules, routing freight to the proper place, and keeping track of the rolling stock. In the early days of railroading, keeping track of all the trains running on the track was not critical, although the railroad tried to keep to a timetable for the benefit of the customers. (MGC.)

Train wrecks were common on the railroad; however, it seems as though the bridges were the main cause. One wreck occurred on Currin Bridge. On June 5, 1909, the steam engine had just crossed the bridge when it started swaying. The railroad bridge collapsed, dumping the coach and freight cars into the river below. In the small town of Cottage Grove, everyone came to help. Thankfully there were only injuries and no deaths. Unfortunately, a second bridge collapsed at Walden, downstream from the Mosby Creek Covered Bridge. This wreck took the lives of the fireman and engineer, who were scalded by steam from the bursting boiler. (Above, CGHS; below, CGM.)

In 1904, the Oregon Pacific and Eastern Railway (OP&E) was known as the Oregon Southeastern Railroad (OS&E). The rail line ran about 18 miles between Cottage Grove and Wildwood. In 1912, OP&E Company incorporated and two years later purchased the OS&E. The OP&E's operations ran for over 16 miles, from an interchange with the Southern Pacific Railroad at Cottage Grove east to Culp Creek. The railway had several wood-burning locomotives, such as the No. 1, No. 3, and No. 9., hauling logs from the mountains to the mills. Best known was the famous "Blue Goose," No. 19, which gave locals and visitors a ride up Row River to one of many stops on the way to the camps. (Above, CGM; below, MGC.)

Engine No. 3 was in service for the Coos Bay Lumber Company before it was moved to Cottage Grove. It is unusual in that the boiler is of saddle-tank design. In 1950, a large storm caused the power transformer at the mill to blow and caused a fire that burned half the mill. The owner Warren H. Daugherty said damage was between $600,000 and $700,000. (MGC.)

Through the hard years, George Gerlinger had tended to the OP&E Railroad while still running his own mill operation in the Willamette Valley. To help the OP&E Railroad survive, he sold some of the locomotives and rolling stock to J. H. Chambers for his logging line just west of Cottage Grove. (MGC.)

Anderson Middleton hauled logs with the "Shay" locomotive, No. 9, down the 3 miles of railroad track that had been built up to Sharps Creek in 1924. The Shay was used by Brown Lumber Company to haul their logs to Disston until 1930, when they eventually closed the line. (MGC.)

The Little Donkey was a small saddle-tank steam engine used by the J. H. Chambers mill to shuttle railcars around the mill. Chambers had several locomotives and his own short line going west towards Lorane. To assure continued access to the short line going east to Culp Creek, he even bought up the failing OP&E Railroad in 1917. (CGHS.)

The Southern Pacific had its beginnings in the Central Pacific Rail Road Company of California in 1861. They built the western portion of the transcontinental railroad from Sacramento to Promontory, Utah. After the completion of the transcontinental line, they began to rapidly expand up the Pacific Coast. At the same time, two railroad companies were formed in Portland with the same name, the Oregon Central Railroad Company; they made little headway until Ben Holladay stepped in and got things moving. The rails reached Roseburg on December 3, 1872, where Holladay ran out of funds. Henry Villard took over and made it to Ashland in 1884. By July 1887, the line was once again out of funds and was acquired under lease by the Southern Pacific, who finished the line from Hornbrook, California, to Ashland on December 17, 1887. (CGHS.)

When the Bohemia mines started to boom in 1902, a short line was built. It ran from Cottage Grove out as far as the town of Disston. The first steam engine to run along this track was engine No. 4, known to the locals as "Old Slow and Easy." The engine was from the Corvallis and Eastern Railroad and ran out to Disston daily. (MGC.)

Cordwood was stacked on a high platform to make for quick transfers to a waiting tender car. Steam engines could be fired on most anything that burned readily. Back east, most engines ran on coal, but out west, early engines were almost exclusively wood burners, although later engines used oil. (CGHS.)

The Oregon Central Railroad was the name of two railroad companies. They both had federal land grants that had been assigned to Oregon State in 1866 to assist in building a line from Portland south into California. The "East Side Company" of Salem (incorporated 1867) eventually received the grant for its line east of the Willamette and was reorganized in 1870 as the Oregon and California Railroad (O&C). They completed the line in 1887. Portland supported the competing "West Side Company" (incorporated 1866), which only built to the McMinnville area and was sold to the O&C in 1880. The O&C was later bought out by the Southern Pacific Company and is part of the Union Pacific Railroad. The West Side line is now operated by the Portland and Western Railroad between Beaverton and Forest Grove. (CGHS.)

The "Blue Goose" on the Oregon Pacific and Eastern rails is pictured here. The old No. 19 was built in 1915 by Baldwin. Weighing in at 87 tons, the boiler proudly wore bullet scars from its service in a Mexican revolution. Later it hauled logs for McCloud River Lumber Company and pulled its share of cars for the Yreka Western Railroad. Bought by the OP&E and put into service as an excursion train in 1971, it served steam-train enthusiasts for many years. (MGC.)

RIDE THE SCENIC OREGON PACIFIC & EASTERN RAILWAY CO.

STEAM EXCURSION TRAIN

THE GOOSE

OLD SLOW AND EASY

A STEAM-POWERED ADVENTURE INTO OREGON'S GREEN CALAPOOYA MOUNTAINS

OREGON PACIFIC & EASTERN

1972 SCHEDULES 1972

"The Goose" Passenger Train
OREGON PACIFIC & EASTERN RAILWAY COMPANY

TIMETABLE

MAY 13 thru JUNE 11 — SATURDAYS, SUNDAYS, HOLIDAYS

Village Green Station	*4	*6
Leaves	10:00 a.m.	2:00 p.m.
Returns	12:15 p.m.	4:15 p.m.
	The Evergreen	The Emerald

DAILY SERVICE
JUNE 12 thru SEPT. 4

Village Green Station	*2	*4	*6
	Daily Mon. thru Fri.	Sat. & Sun. Only	Sat. & Sun. Only
Leaves	1:00 p.m.	10:00 a.m.	2:00 p.m.
Returns	3:15 p.m.	12:15 p.m.	4:15 p.m.
	The Diesel Row River	The Evergreen	The Emerald

SEPT. 5 thru OCT. 1 — SAT. & SUN. ONLY

Village Green Station	*4	*6
	Sat. & Sun	Sat. & Sun
Leaves	10:00 a.m.	2:00 p.m.
Returns	12:15 p.m.	4:15 p.m.
	The Evergreen	The Emerald

FARES - ROUND TRIP

$ 3.90	Adults		Children
2.75	Juniors 12 yrs. thru 17 yrs.		Under 5 yrs.
1.50	Children 5 yrs. thru 11 yrs.		No Charge

EQUIPMENT

COACHES
DOME LOUNGE (Cocktails)
Bedroom Suite or Drawing Room - $5.00 extra per party 1 to 5 persons
LUNCH LOUNGE (Refreshments)
MOUNTAIN OBSERVATION

Reservations Suggested
OREGON PACIFIC & EASTERN RY. CO.
P. O. BOX 565 ● COTTAGE GROVE, OREGON 97424 ● AREA 503-942-3368

The tickets read, "The fun line. The goose will take you over her long-past working route . . . a century back in time." The need to get freight and ore in and out of the Bohemia mining district spurred a rail line to be built, and the Oregon Securities Company was formed. On Memorial Day 1902, Gov. Theodore Geer was there to help drive in the final spike. Throughout the years, the line got the nickname "the old slow and easy." (MGC.)

"The Goose" was a steam engine that lived a full life. After many years of hauling logs from the mountains to the mills, the engine took on a new life. In the mid-1900s, the train began pulling passenger cars instead of heavy log cars. It had its second inaugural run on Memorial Day. Oregon's governor Tom McCall came down to drive the final spike into the railroad. (MGC.)

"The Goose" ride started at the local depot, the Village Green. It became one of the best-known historical rides in the area. After leaving the depot, one could ride through the mountains and see a few sawmills, a couple beautiful covered bridges, Dorena Lake, the Indian marriage tree, and much more. (MGC.)

In 1926, Buster Keaton chose Cottage Grove for the location of his silent Civil War epic, *The General*. It is said to be one of the greatest silent comedies of all time. Keaton spent $40,000, which included building a trestle in only 10 days and purchasing three steam engines for his movie. There could be no rehearsals for the famous crash scene, so they took one shot and one shot only. Keaton tried to lure several men to ride on the train and then jump off the runaway train at the right time by offering them $500, but there were no takers. So Buster was forced to use dummies in the scene instead. (CGHS.)

Pile drivers were used to pound logs into the ground, providing support for the railroad track. The term also referred to members of the construction crew who worked with pile driving rigs. One traditional type of pile driver involves a heavy weight placed between guides so that it is able to freely slide up and down in a single line. It is placed upon a pile and the weight is raised—which may involve the use of hydraulics, steam diesel, or even manual labor. When the weight reaches its highest point, it is then released and smashes down like a giant hammer, driving the piling into the ground. Ancient pile driving equipment used manual or animal labor to lift heavy weights, usually by means of pulleys, to drop the weight onto the end of the piling. (Right, MGC; below, CGM.)

Visit us at
arcadiapublishing.com

www.ingramcontent.com/pod-product-compliance
Lightning Source LLC
Chambersburg PA
CBHW080616110426
42813CB00006B/1522

* 9 7 8 1 5 3 1 6 5 3 1 6 3 *